5 INSTAGRAM GRO STRATEGY

How You Can Train the Algorithm to Show Your Content to More People, Increase Your Followers, And 10× Your Content Engagement.

DAVID DARBY

Table of Contents

INTRODUCTION

Dear friend,

You're about to learn that this guide is not only simple to follow, but it will also deliver on its promises regarding the mistake you have to avoid.

After spending over 4 years monitoring how social media platforms work, I've come to notice that a lot of changes happen day after day. However, there are some underlying principles that if understood, leveraging social media for your business and/or personal brand's growth in terms of impact, influence, and income will be easy for you IRRESPECTIVE of these regular changes. A quick question...

Trying to open a gate with the key or trying to open it by breaking it down, which will be easier and save you time? It definitely will be using the key. The same thing applies to social media. Tons of people are trying to get into the compound (grow their brands, make sales, build communities, and so on), but because they don't have the key (a practical guide from someone with years of intentional study and real experience from experimentations), they spend a lot of time breaking the gate before they see the result.

This is why the process is hard for a lot of people, and most even quit before they break down the gate.

In this guide you will get to know why Instagram is important most especially if you're a small business owner, or a brand. You will learn the most effective strategies, how to identify your audience, defining your buyer persona (or customer) journey as well setting goals and tracking your growth.

I am already excited that you're here. Do well to also refer to the guide at any point of help.

CHAPTER 1

INSTGRAM GROWTH STRATEGY

An Instagram growth strategy refers to a deliberate plan of action aimed at increasing the number of followers, engagement, and overall reach on the platform. It involves setting goals, developing a content strategy, engaging with followers, leveraging Instagram features, and analyzing metrics to track progress.

Having an Instagram growth strategy is crucial for businesses that want to succeed on the platform. Without a clear plan of action, businesses risk losing out to competitors who have a well-defined strategy. A growth strategy ensures that businesses can effectively reach and engage with their target audience, and ultimately achieve their business objectives.

An Instagram growth strategy is a comprehensive plan of action designed to increase the number of followers, engagement, and overall reach of a business or individual on the platform. It involves setting specific goals, developing a content strategy, engaging with followers, leveraging Instagram features, and analyzing metrics to track progress.

Having a clear Instagram growth strategy is critical to the success of any business or individual on the platform. The strategy should be designed to achieve specific objectives, such as increasing brand awareness, driving traffic to a website, or generating sales.

1.1 Importance of having an Instagram growth strategy

There are several reasons why having an Instagram growth strategy is essential:

1. Increased visibility: A well-planned Instagram growth strategy can help increase the visibility of a business or individual on the platform, resulting in more followers, engagement, and reach.

2. Targeted audience engagement: A growth strategy can help businesses engage with their target audience more effectively, resulting in increased brand loyalty and potential sales.

3. Improved brand awareness: A growth strategy can help businesses establish a clear brand identity and voice on the platform, making it easier for followers to recognize and engage with their content.

4. Competitive advantage: Having a well-defined Instagram growth strategy can provide a competitive advantage over businesses that do not have a clear plan of action, helping to stand out in a crowded marketplace.

5. Measurable results: By setting specific goals and tracking metrics, a growth strategy can help businesses measure the effectiveness of

their efforts and make data-driven decisions to optimize their strategy for continued success.

CHAPTER 2

AUDIENCE IDENTIFICATION

Identifying and understanding your target audience is a critical aspect of any effective Instagram growth strategy. By developing a clear understanding of your audience's demographics, interests, behaviors, and pain points, you can tailor your content strategy and engagement tactics to better meet their needs and preferences, ultimately resulting in increased engagement and followers.

One effective way to understand your audience is by developing buyer personas, which are fictional representations of your ideal customer. A buyer persona takes into account demographic information such as age, gender, and location, as well as psychographic information such as values, beliefs, and interests.

2.1   Defining the Buyer Persona Journey

The buyer persona journey is a framework for understanding the various stages that a potential customer goes through when considering a purchase. By mapping out this journey, you can better understand the needs and pain points of your audience at each stage and develop content that speaks to those needs.

The buyer persona journey typically consists of the following stages:

1. Awareness: At this stage, the potential customer becomes aware of a problem or need that they have.

2. Consideration: The potential customer begins to research and consider various solutions to their problem.

3. Decision: The potential customer makes a decision to purchase a specific product or service.

2.3 Creating A Buyer Persona

Creating a buyer persona involves conducting research to gather information about your target audience and using that information to create a fictional representation of your ideal customer.

Here are the steps to create a buyer persona:

1. Conduct research: Gather information about your target audience through various methods such as surveys, interviews, and social media analytics. Some key areas to focus on include demographics (age, gender, location), psychographics (values, beliefs, interests), and behaviors (buying habits, social media usage).

2. Analyze the data: Once you have gathered the necessary information, analyze the data to identify patterns and trends. Look for commonalities among your audience to determine what motivates them, what challenges they face, and what solutions they are seeking.

3. Create a fictional character: Based on the research and analysis, create a fictional character that represents your ideal customer. Give the persona a name, job title, and personal details such as hobbies and interests.

4. Define the persona's goals and challenges: Identify the persona's goals and challenges related to your product or service. What are they hoping to achieve by using your product or service, and what obstacles are they facing in achieving those goals?

5. Identify the persona's pain points: What are the persona's biggest frustrations and pain points related to your product or service? What are their objections and concerns that might prevent them from making a purchase?

6. Develop messaging and content: Use the information gathered from the buyer persona to create messaging and content that speaks to their needs and preferences. Tailor your content to address their pain points and offer solutions that resonate with their goals and challenges.

Tips: Creating a buyer persona takes time and effort, but it can be a valuable tool for understanding your target audience and tailoring your marketing efforts to meet their needs. By understanding your audience and their motivations, you can create content and engagement tactics that resonate with them and ultimately drive increased engagement, followers, and sales on Instagram.

CHAPTER 3

GOAL SETTING

3.1 Setting Instagram Goals

Setting specific, measurable, achievable, relevant, and time-bound (SMART) goals is the foundation of any effective Instagram growth strategy. SMART goals provide a clear direction and focus for your efforts on the platform, helping you to achieve your objectives more effectively;

Identifying Specific, Measurable, Achievable, Relevant, and Time-bound (SMART) Goals:

1. Specific: Your Instagram goals should be clearly defined and specific to your business or individual objectives. For example, increasing the number of followers, boosting engagement rates, or driving traffic to your website.

2. Measurable: Your goals should be measurable, allowing you to track progress and analyze the effectiveness of your efforts. This can include metrics such as follower growth, engagement rates, reach, and website traffic.

3. Achievable: Your goals should be realistic and achievable within a given timeframe, based on your available resources and the current state of your Instagram account.

4. Relevant: Your goals should be relevant to your overall business or individual objectives and align with your brand identity and voice on the platform.

5. Time-bound: Your goals should have a specific timeframe for achievement, such as increasing followers by a certain percentage within three months.

3.2   Understanding Your Audience

To effectively set SMART goals, it's essential to understand your target audience on Instagram. This includes their demographics, interests, and behaviors on the platform.

By understanding your audience, you can tailor your content strategy and engagement tactics to better meet their needs and preferences, ultimately resulting in increased engagement and followers.

In the next chapter and beyond, we will be going deeper into these strategies and how to effectively apply them.

CHAPTER 4

HASHTAGS STRATEGY

Hashtags are commonly used in posts, to reach more targeted users within your Niche. Use hashtags to categorize your content and make it easier for users to find your posts.

Let me ask you this question, how effective have hashtags been in your account? Have you been able to reach thousands of people or get the desired results you always wanted from hashtags? Probably not and that is one of the reasons you are going through this right now. I have gotten almost a million reach on my video; from hashtags, this was a personal and viral video mixed together. Now what is the difference between yours and mine? People when researching for hashtags just pick randomly from Instagram or Google, whatever carries the Keyword they are looking for. But that is totally wrong, whenever you have a post and you are looking for hashtags for your posts, there is something called HASHTAGS STACKING.

4.1. Hashtag Stacking

Hashtags stacking is an Act where you pick Low, Medium, and High post counts hashtags, and use them to rank among hashtags. Instagram limits you to using 30 tags per post, but it's not recommended to use all

30 spots especially frequently, as the Instagram algorithm bot tends to mark it as spam, and it might reduce the Trust score of your account. Now what is recommended? 15, 20 Hashtags. You can decide to use 25 that's okay and 30 can be used once in a while. I recommend 15 to 20 Hashtags though. Picking 5 Low hashtags around 100k to 300k post counts, another 5 between 500k to 800k post counts, and another 5 from 1 to 2Million Post counts. Why Hashtag Stacking? With hashtags stacking, when you are able to rank on low post tags, it pushes your content and help rank in the medium post count hashtags and that pushes your content to rank in High post counts hashtags. This might take time a bit when researching, but it's totally worth it.

TIPS: For Viral posts, you can put your hashtags in your caption. But if you love to make a neater caption, put your hashtags in your comment section. It still works as both have been effective for me.

CHAPTER 5

LINK IN BIO/LOGO STRATEGY

If you have a website and you are not utilizing your Instagram with it then you are doing it totally wrong, or you just fill the website spot with the random long link, then you still are doing it wrong. People love neatness not just in the house but also online on social media. I Have seen pages post links like this "https://www.facebook.com/profile.php?id=100004389976166" either redirects to their Facebook, YouTube or even a blog.

An example is these ones, a good way how it should look with a perfect logo blend.

If you have to redirect traffic to a page, that has a long link like the URL above, it is recommended that you purchase a Domain name, they cost a bit low and are inexpensive ranging from $3.99 to $9.99

depending on the domain. If you can't afford to purchase one or feel it's not necessary, then be free to use a URL shortener such as Bit.ly or Google URL shortener. If you have a store and you have an Instagram page for it with the URL on your Bio, whenever you make a post always use a call to Action at the end of your caption if promoting a product, with (LINK IN BIO). People love it when things are easily done or when they are given directions on l how to go about certain things.

Every good business has a Logo, Your Instagram page, should be your business also. Many people just take a random whacked ass Image (apologies for my Language couldn't find a better way of describing it) and upload it in their Bio as a profile picture, people want to hang around pros, and a bad logo can result in bad follow conversion. Lots of people feel like their profile picture plays no role in converting followers who visit their profile page, but it does a lot. If I see an action from a page liking or commenting on my post and has a good logo and username, I would be curious to check out their page, and in turn, if I love what I see follow them. Now where do you get a good logo from?

I recommend paying a graphics designer some charge anywhere between $5 to $10 for a good logo. You can check www.upwork.com, or www.fiverr.com for a good logo creator. Or if you are on a tight budget then you can make one for yourself on www.canva.com. Be sure to have your page name on your logo if it's a short name or at least.

TIPS: I would recommend your check out Google for a good logo composition as well as types.

CHAPTER 6

STORIES STRATEGY

Instagram Stories have skyrocketed in the past 12 Months, with Instagram adding changes and lots of features to using stories, Including hashtags, Polls, and Q&A on Story posts. One thing people do when making story post includes numerous Hashtags up to 5 to 10 hashtags, and then other features make the post, crowded with unnecessary things. Yes, hashtags are great but, covering up all stories with hashtags won't help you rank and expose your stories to more viewers.

I recommend using a maximum of three in a story and mostly 1 or 2 hashtags in a story. You can make it rank on a sub-niche hashtag instead of a wide huge one, that's another mistake people tend to make. For example, if you have a travel page, instead of using the hashtag #Travel in your story, you can narrow it down, to #VanTravel (if your post is about people who travel in a van).

Always Narrow it down when you are on a small page, and making story posts gets more traction than using a very wide tag and trying to rank on it, it's very difficult ranking on huge tags when you are on a very small page. Polls. Always use polls in your stories and ask questions. Asking questions in your stories helps to push them to rank in Hashtags explore when people start interacting with your hashtags, it tells the Instagram bot that your post, has got value in it, and It's worthy to be seen by others.

TIP: When you post things of different niches in your stories, they also help go Viral let's say you run a viral Page, and post things about funny dogs or DIY videos. This was proven by people who get over 30k views on Stories in the person of Jordan Shepherd and Lamar Neflone.

CHAPTER 7

INSTAGRAM ADS STRATEGY

The importance of using Instagram ads is a great way to reach a wider audience and attract new followers. It's not a must you run ads on the basis of the product or services you offer but on one particular thing *"To reach a wider audience/ follower as well as grow in your niche"* At least you do this once every six (6) months.

Instagram ads can be highly targeted, ensuring that your content is seen by people who are likely to be interested in your products or services.

Benefits of using Instagram ads There are several benefits to using Instagram ads, including:

1. Increased reach: Instagram ads allow you to reach a wider audience than organic content alone.
2. Highly targeted: Instagram ads can be highly targeted based on factors such as demographics, interests, and behaviors.
3. Cost-effective: Instagram ads can be cost-effective, especially if you target your ads effectively.
4. Measurable: Instagram ads are measurable, allowing you to track the performance of your ads and make adjustments as needed.

By implementing these Instagram growth strategies, you can increase your visibility and attract new followers to your account.

TIPS: for using Instagram ads

- Use Instagram's built-in ad platform to create highly targeted ads.
- Experiment with different ad formats, such as Stories ads or carousel ads.
- Monitor your ad performance and adjust your targeting and messaging as needed.

CHAPTER 8

VIRAL CONTENT STRATEGY (FOR REPOST PAGES)

Viral contents are videos or Images, that have gone viral before on Instagram. Yes, very simple. These are the kind of content you repost on your pages to go viral, lots of people make the mistake of just going to the explore page and reposting whatever is seen there as far as it has over 100 thousand views. A video can have 100k views but still perform low. There are factors you have to consider, before reposting a video from the Explore page.

Below are some of the factors:

• Videos should be over 800k to 1M views.

• Pictures on explore pages must be over 20k likes within the past 24Hrs

• If reposting from a small page such as a page with 10 to 100k followers, make sure the video has over 500k views with a catching cover/thumbnail.

8.1 How to find viral Content from a specific page in your Niche?

Whenever you visit a page go through the last 30 posts or 20 posts look at the average engagement on each post and find the video/image with 4x or 5x or even 10x the usual engagements. This is how you pick your viral content. Most of these posts might not have hashtags in them, meaning these pages are using a different way other than hashtags to go viral. If you happen to find hashtags in the viral post which you would love to repost, then I recommend you take those hashtags and use them as well. Do not try to reinvent the wheel it's very easy to be successful in a business someone has already done by copying it than trying to complicate it by re-inventing the wheel same goes for Instagram as well.

CONCLUSION

Utilizing effective growth strategies is crucial for achieving success on Instagram. By implementing the five growth strategies discussed, including optimizing your profile, creating high-quality content, engaging with your followers, using hashtags, and using Instagram ads, you can attract new followers and increase engagement with your content. Each strategy requires consistency, attention to detail, and a willingness to experiment and adapt to achieve the desired results. By committing to these strategies, you can build a strong and engaged Instagram following that supports your business or personal brand. Remember, growth on Instagram is a continuous process, so stay focused and stay committed to achieving your goals.

Additionally, it's important to keep in mind that the success of your Instagram growth strategies also relies on your ability to understand your audience and their preferences. By regularly analyzing your Instagram insights and engagement metrics, you can identify the types of content that resonate with your audience and adjust your strategies accordingly.

Furthermore, consistency is key when it comes to implementing growth strategies on Instagram. It's not enough to simply apply these strategies once and hope for the best. You need to consistently produce high-quality content, engage with your followers, use relevant hashtags, and monitor your performance metrics to ensure that you're on track to achieve your goals.

Finally, it's worth noting that Instagram is constantly evolving, and what works today may not work tomorrow. To stay ahead of the game, it's essential to stay up to date with the latest trends and updates on the platform. By staying informed and adapting your strategies accordingly, you can continue to grow and succeed on Instagram.

Printed in Great Britain
by Amazon